The Nig
Larry Kramer
Kissed Me

The Night Larry Kramer Kissed Me

David Drake

Foreword by Michelangelo Signorile

Anchor Books
Doubleday
New York London Toronto Sydney Auckland

AN ANCHOR BOOK
PUBLISHED BY DOUBLEDAY
a division of
Bantam Doubleday Dell Publishing Group, Inc.
1540 Broadway, New York, New York 10036

ANCHOR BOOKS, DOUBLEDAY, and the portrayal of an anchor
are trademarks of Doubleday,
a division of Bantam Doubleday Dell Publishing Group, Inc.

Photographs by William Gibson/Martha Swope Associates

Book Design by Gretchen Achilles

Library of Congress Cataloging-in-Publication Data

Drake, David, 1963–
The night Larry Kramer kissed me / David Drake ; foreword by
Michelangelo Signorile.
p.   cm.
1. Gay men—United States—Drama.   I. Title.
PS3554.R1962N5   1994
812´.54—dc20   93-21339
                                                          CIP

ISBN 0-385-47204-8
Copyright © 1992 by David Drake
Introduction copyright © 1994 by David Drake
Foreword copyright © 1994 by Michelangelo Signorile
All Rights Reserved
Printed in the United States of America
First Anchor Books Edition: March 1994

10 9 8 7 6 5 4 3 2 1

To Sean Strub
for creating a place in the world for me
to tell the truth.

And to Chuck Brown
for leading me there.

Contents

Acknowledgments

Most sincere gratitude must be acknowledged to all those who gave me their support, guidance, and love throughout the process of bringing this play to an audience:

Dick Scanlan, Adele Bove, Ron Brown Grayson, Dave Drakula, Doris Drake, Jim Morgan, Tim Hunter, Ray Schilke, Ali Sherwin, Jon Winkelman, ACT UP/New York, ACT UP/Baltimore, Ellie Covan and Dixon Place, Jose Villarubia, David Grimm, Arnold Engelman and Westbeth Theatre Center, Jed Mattes, Jim Griffith, Christopher Makos, Bob Mueller, Michael Wakefield, Michelangelo Signorile, Stephen Gendin, Loretta Grande, Robert Knapp, Maryrose Wood, Tammis Day, Richard Boyce, Ken Johnson, Susanne Tighe/Boneau Bryan-Brown, Kathy Haberthur and Philip Rinaldi, Tom Viola, Andrew P. Tobias, Yoko Ono, Ed Wintle, Howard Grossman, Queer Nation, Marvin Shulman, Rodger MacFarlane, Victor Zonanna, Richard Feldman, Simon Halls, Peter Vanderwicken, Max Westerman, Cyril Brosnan, Peter Neufeld, Chris Buck, Steve McGraw's, Gay and Lesbian Community Center of New York, Elliot Bertoni, Life on the Water Theatre (S.F., CA.), Tiffany Theatre (L.A., CA.), Stuart Berger, Eric Paeper, Charles Ching, Sean Strub, Chuck Brown, William Gibson/Martha Swope & Associates, my Doubleday editor Bruce Tracy, Martha Levin, Peter Hagan, Steve Sandberg, Victor Latino, Mark Redanty, Marc Holzman, The Flirtations, and Larry Kramer.

Foreword

To experience David Drake's *The Night Larry Kramer Kissed Me* is to bear witness to an explosion that has occurred in the gay and lesbian community in America.

Author and playwright Larry Kramer was among those who lit the fuse. In 1987, Kramer gave an impassioned speech to an audience at the Lesbian and Gay Community Services Center in New York City. He attacked the government for its negligent response to the AIDS plague, chided his audience of gay men and lesbians for not venting their rage, and made an urgent call to action.

The small band of individuals who took up Kramer's call formed a group committed to direct action and civil disobedience to end the AIDS crisis: ACT UP—the AIDS Coalition to Unleash Power. The group's brash public demonstrations were immediately controversial but immensely effective at drawing attention to the epidemic. Its membership soon mushroomed, and chapters rose up in cities and towns around the country.

Those of us who worked within ACT UP in New York at the time could not have imagined the far-reaching effects that our political organizing would have. We did not end the AIDS crisis, as many of us believed we would; the ravages of AIDS are in fact worse now than ever before, and government inaction is still mainly to blame.

But ACT UP did send a jolt through all of American society, a message that something was dreadfully wrong. The mainstream media were pushed to look at the epidemic more often and with a bit more insight. Government was forced to at least address the issue. The Food and Drug Administration and the National Institutes of Health reexamined their glacial bureaucracies and began to streamline some policies. Political candidates were put on the spot about AIDS and felt hard-pressed to make promises to AIDS activists.

Most significantly, ACT UP moved perhaps hundreds of thousands of complacent gay men and lesbians around the country to action. It gave courage to those who were frightened, invigorated those who were morally and spiritually drained, and brought scores of men and women out of the closet, convincing them that the most forceful way to fight AIDS was to put a face on a community that had been decimated by it. ACT UP brought to the queer individual, perhaps for the first time, a sense of responsibility to his or her community. After two years, ACT UP spawned the equally brazen Queer Nation, a group determined to rout the closet out of American culture.

But perhaps ACT UP's greatest impact was its most subtle. In the first pivotal years of ACT UP's existence, from 1987 through 1991, the group was a sort of finishing school for many of us who, through magazines, books, films, art and theater, would take its powerful message far and wide in the years to come.

Like Tony Kushner with his Broadway hit *Angels in America*, and like Kramer himself with his 1992 critically acclaimed Off-Broadway play *The Destiny of Me*, David Drake is one of those who took that message to the stage. In *The Night Larry Kramer Kissed Me* Drake masterfully articulates ACT UP's most provocative mantra: Turn anger into action. The play is infused with fury over the AIDS crisis, over gay-bashing and over homophobia, and it challenges the audience to take that passion and do something constructive with it.

But also like ACT UP, rather than continually foisting gloom on his audience or, worse yet, lecturing them into oblivion, Drake utilizes brilliant wit and boyish style to fire his compelling missive. It makes for a commanding and demanding yet highly entertaining look at contemporary gay life.

It is in fact with his sense of humor that this talented man coaxes us to take a serious look at him and at ourselves. Drake prods gay men to examine our true motivations in pieces like "Why I Go to the Gym" and "12″ Single," while at the same time allowing us to laugh at our often ridiculous behavior. In the "The Birthday Triptych: The Night Larry Kramer Kissed Me," we learn of Drake's first actions after seeing Larry Kramer's landmark play *The Normal Heart* in 1985 and after being filled with fear and rage over the *New York Times*' scant coverage of AIDS—before he finally joined ACT UP: "I ran for days to escape the invisible, unprintable killer," he tells us. "I ran for a fantasy. I ran for a fix. I ran for *42nd Street:* The Musical." And, while *The Night Larry Kramer Kissed Me* is imbued with a sense of gay history, Drake takes us on a romp into the future that surely feeds some of our darker fantasies, complete with the assassination of Rush Limbaugh, the imprisonment of Phyllis Schlafly, and, my own personal favorite, the outing of Siskel & Ebert.

Perhaps most importantly, David Drake is fiercely out of the closet and unapologetic. Those who see or read *The Night Larry Kramer Kissed Me* witness a proud, young, gay man who is fighting back. And millions of people—including gay teens in search of validation—who have read Drake's reviews, seen him on television talk shows or perused through the countless newspapers and magazines that have featured him, have seen a queer role model for our times. In that way, *The Night Larry Kramer Kissed Me* is a coming-of-age story for a new queer generation, and Drake, with clarity and humor, makes this generation's central point: Coming out of the closet is a necessity for everyone. Not only is it the most important action a person can take for his or her community at this crucial period in time, but it is the most powerful thing a person can do for his or her own, personal well-being.

That is the message—the message of the ACT UP, the message of Larry Kramer—with which David Drake himself now "kisses" thousands of people across America.

—Michelangelo Signorile

Introduction

Getting out of the closet is a journey in and of itself. Staying out is another. But where do you go from there? Where is "out"? What are the obstacles that you face? Where do they come from? How do you overcome them? What is the source of your commitment to staying out? How deep does it run?

Being out—and positioning yourself to move forward—takes a sense of self-worth rarely chronicled for queer people. My will to move forward came from a belief in my gut that I was of real value. That being gay really was good. The personal quest of my life and work has been to articulate the truth of this belief.

What guides this quest is hope—a hope to find my emotional and spiritual kinship to other gay and lesbian people.

The stories that chronicle the journey that is *The Night Larry Kramer Kissed Me* started flying out of me in the summer of 1990. AIDS had taken the lives of several of my friends. I cried. I grieved. I went numb. The AIDS crisis had matured into a full-blown epidemic. Of the number of people I counted in my circle of friends still living, the majority were HIV+. This wasn't going away. My numbness went flat. My helplessness hit bottom. My anger was born.

I was fortunate to have found a place to channel my emotions effectively in the AIDS Coalition To Unleash Power. These people were gathered with one purpose: to end the epidemic. Week after week I attended ACT UP's general meetings at New York's Gay and Lesbian Community Center on West Thirteenth Street. As I tried to process the enormous amount of information spewing forth, it was—as I describe in "A Thousand Points of Light"—a "hurricane of clarity." I didn't know it in those first few months, but I was learning how to separate and clarify the context and content of the issues that had built the AIDS epidemic. ACT UP's urgent objective, and its manner of achieving that objective, set the standard by which this play would be written, performed, and produced. We didn't have time to waste. Our people were dying.

ACT UP's determined focus to ending the epidemic spawned another direct-action group that spring of 1990—Queer Nation. If ACT UP had taught us the political disease that continued to spread AIDS—power, money, and class structure—then Queer Nation set out to tackle the social disease that informed it: homophobia. By *promoting* homosexuality, Queer Nation's agenda defied everything the closet was structured around. QN did this with fabulousness and ferocity. They allowed me to embrace the brutalness and the beauty at the core of my truth: sissy boy shame—and rage.

Being a sissy boy was the root of my self-hatred. It was the ugliest thing in my closet. As a matter of fact, it was what my closet had been built around. Sissy-ness is the most pronounced stereotype in the catalogue of homosexual male references. It is the margin by which gay men's worth is valued in society. Boys who act that way are criticized, embarrassed, bullied, even murdered. Feminine behavior is not encouraged in boys, or even tolerated. It is loathed. It is actively sought out by straight society to be hidden, removed, or destroyed.

The naming and claiming of the truth of my oppression is how I came to realize that although I wasn't living with HIV in my blood, I was living with it in my life. AIDS is a very real viral disease. It is also the outgrowth of a hatred that informs the care of queer people's health. Active homophobia created AIDS.

But I had known this for some time. The content and context of the AIDS epidemic had been introduced to me on June 27, 1985, the night I saw Larry Kramer's play *The Normal Heart* at the New York Shakespeare Festival's Public Theater. That experience eventually led me to ACT UP. It would also lead me to accept the truth of my shame, which enabled me to accept the truth of my goodness as a gay man. And ultimately, to bonding with my tribe—and to the fury of intention that spun these stories out of my queer soul.

Silence = Death.

David Drake
Los Angeles
August 1993

The Stories

The Birthday Triptych
"Somewhere . . ."
"Out There in the Night"
"The Night Larry Kramer Kissed Me"

Owed to the Village People, Part One

Why I Go to the Gym

12˝ Single

Owed to the Village People, Part Two

A Thousand Points of Light

". . . and *The Way We Were*"

The Birthday Triptych

"Somewhere . . ."

My sixth birthday,
June 27, 1969.
The night the Stonewall Riots
erupted onto the Village streets
in New York City.

The night I sat gripped,
glued to the edge of my seat
as the stage of the Baltimore County Community Theater
erupted with a story
that was also happening live.
Erupted with a story
also of the streets of New York
right in front of my 6-year-old eyes.
As that Baltimore County Community Theater stage
erupted with *West Side Story*!

(The opening musical phrase of the West Side Story
prologue is heard. Performer watches the show unfold,
describing it as he speaks.)

    with gangs & cops & switchblades & rape
    & rumbles & bullets & big black wigs

& screaming & fighting & singing & dancing
& dancing & dancing & dancing & dancing
& dancing & dancing & dancing & dancing & love
    & kisses
    & blood.

        Somewhere.

End of Part One.

The Birthday Triptych

"Out There in the Night"

My 16th birthday,
June 27, 1979.
The night I held
two theater tickets
in my hand:
one for me
and one for him:
Tim.
The Older Man.
Seventeen.
Swim Team Tim.
Debate Team Tim.
Title role in the spring musical *Pippin* Tim.

    Yeah, that one.

The one I had never been totally alone with
until this night.
Now driving me crazy with the scent
of that clorine-bleached hair
filling the air,
driving me crazy all the way

into downtown Baltimore
to see that show,
that show I'd wanted to see so,
so badly.
To see those stories of Broadway Gypsies.
To hear those stories of New York City
come to life
from behind each 8-by-10 glossy
in *A Chorus Line.*

(Opening musical phrase of "God I Hope I Get It" from
A Chorus Line *is heard. Performer watches the show*
unfold, describing it as he speaks.)

God, I really loved it.
I really loved it.
How many nights I'd spent locked alone
in my room
with the original cast album
that I had memorized.
Singing & dancing & singing & dancing
& dancing & dancing & dancing & dancing to the sounds
now happening LIVE
right in front of my 16-year-old eyes.
Surprised by the stories
between the songs.
The stories
not heard
on the album.
The album that gave me no warning that one story

would appear,
told on the stage
all alone
that was not my story

but was my story.

Out of the mouth
of that Puerto Rican, dancer-boy "Paul"
telling the story
of a boy
who loves boys.
A story that had seeped
into my childhood sleep at 7,
8,
9,
10,
11,
12,
13,
14,
15,
now 16,
hiding my swollen eyes from him,
Tim,
at my side
driving
silently
through the night
on the highway.

Driving home
to be alone
with the embarrassment of this exposing moment;
displayed on my tear-smeared, red-blushed face.
Displayed
        in front of him.
        Tim.

Ignition clicked off.
Engine stopped.
Parked in the driveway—
        watching the fluorescent blue television glow
        silently explode
        through the living room's lace-curtained
        bay window.
"I gotta go," I said.
"No, wait," he said. "You'd better wipe your face,"
        as he gave me the white handkerchief
        from his blue blazer pocket.

"Thank you, Tim."

"So, I guess you know . . .
that Puerto Rican boy in the show
is like me.
I'm like that."

"I know," he said. "And I like that,"
        as he reached across the bucket seats
        taking a hold of my tear-smeared cheeks

to gently place upon my 16-year-old lips
one singularly sensational "ooo, sigh" kiss.
Porch light.
Car door.
"DAD!"

Living room light explosions,
eruptions,
discussions
held behind the lace-curtained bay window
all through the night.
Held
very far away
from what had happened out there
in the driveway.
Held
far away
from what had happened out there
in that story
told from the stage.
Held
far, far away
from what must be allowed to happen
somewhere out there in the night.
Somewhere
out there
far, far, far away
from my sweet 16-year-old birthday sight.

They said, "You can't be gay."

David Drake   10

I said, "I am."

They said, "It's a phase."

I said, "I don't think so."

They said, "Well, even if you were gay,
which you are not!
We don't care.
We don't care.
We really don't care."

And I said, "Well, I do."

Which blew their arms and voices through the roof.

"Oh, great, great.
Now what are we supposed to do?
You know, there's a place for people like you!"

"Yeah,

New York."

End of Part Two.

The Birthday Triptych

"The Night Larry Kramer Kissed Me"

My 22nd birthday,
June 27, 1985.
The night I went to see a play—
one that I'd heard was gay—
that held the promise
of a real live kiss
from a real
live
Brad Davis
upon the lips
of a real live man.

That's the kiss
that I wanted to see.
But not the one that stayed
and stayed
and stayed with me
after June 27, 1985:
The night Larry Kramer kissed me
    with his play
    The Normal Heart.

. . .

That shot through a loose-cannon mouth
and exploded my soul
into a thousand teardrop deaths;
leaving my eyes bruised
from the damp fingerprints
off of my Public Theater Playbill,
and from the cradling palms that smeared
my snot-run-face
with black-ink-blood.

The same stains I wiped daily
from my *New York Times* hands
    and face.
From the pages,
pages,
pages I snapped past
to find the news.
All the news that wasn't there on A1,
    2,
    3,
    4,
    5,
    6,
    7,
    8,
    9,
    10,
    11,
    12,
    13,

14,
15,
16,
17,
18,
19,
20,
21,
22.
On B1,
2,
3,
4,
5,
6,
7,
8,
9,
10,
11,
12,
13,
14,
15,
16,
17,
18.
That was not fit on C1,
2,
3,

4,
5,
6,
7,
8,
9,
10,
11,
12,
13,
14,
15,
16,
17,
18.
To print on D1,
2,
3,
4,
5,
6,
7,
8,
9,
10,
11,
STOP:
"Ballet Dancer,
32,
DEAD."

The night after the night Larry Kramer kissed me
I threw down those pages,
pages,
pages from my *New York Times*
and ran for days to escape the invisible,
unprintable
killer

     stalking me?

I ran for a fantasy.
I ran for a fix.
I ran for *42nd Street:*
     The Musical.
Slamming the gilded doors
on the news,
all the news that had never appeared,
or rather
     disappeared
as house lights fade to black . . .

     KICK!
     BALL!
     CHANGE!
Pretty quickly Pretty Ladies are squealing
with Warner Brothers glee.
A circus of cotton candy wigs bob perkily
back & forth, up & down:
"We're in the moneeeeeeeeeeeeeeeeeeyyyyy!"
"Skies are sunnyyyyyyyyyyyyyyyyyyyyyyyyyyyy!"

"Honeeeeeeeeeeeeeeeeeeeyyyyyyyyyyyyyyyyy!"
Time-Stepping meeeeeeeeeeeeeeeeeeeeeeeee!
all the way to The Lullaby.
Listen
to
The Lullaby.
The Lullaby, baby,
that don't sleep tight
until the dawn.
The Lullaby
that floats
the depression
away.

CLAP!CLAP!CLAP!
House lights.
Exit.
Broadway.

The Lullaby haunts me home.

The week
after the night
after the night
after the night Larry Kramer kissed me
The Lullaby of rest
would not sleep with me;
        only the missing breaths of lovers,
        tricks,
        (anyone)

moaning into,
warming up on,
sliding down on
ice-thin sheets.

The month
after the night
after the night
after the night
after the night
after the night Larry Kramer kissed me
my heart wouldn't stop letting me lie
        awake;
        terrorized with shortness of breath,
        with shortness of life
        gone by-
        bye, baby
        with The Lullaby.
        The Lullaby.
        The Lullaby that never put anyone to sleep
        gently
        into any night
        or day.

Hey, hey, hey,
good night, baby.
Sleep tight, baby.
Milkman's on his way . . .
        to SMASH
        and SPLATTER

David Drake   20

his carton upon the wicked stage,
on your FACE, baby,
yeah, sleep TIGHT
with The Lullaby.
The Lullaby.
The Lullaby that swelled
and swelled
and swelled
and swelled for year
after year
after year
after year
after month
after month
after week
after week
after night
after night
after night
after night
after The Night Larry Kramer Kissed Me
with his smacking SWAK
that hurled me out
onto the street
and into the folded arms
of a *New York Times* Nation
that refused to embrace my snot-run-face.
Yeah, it was The Night Larry Kramer Kissed Me
that I stood dazed,
single

in the street.
Public Theater Playbill
twisting in my fist.
Waiting for the others
who had also been kissed.
Watching for the others
whose faces were bruised
with Black-Ink-Blood.
And listening
to The Lullaby
that I've stood
ENOUGH
OF!

Until this dawn . . .

when I hear the early voices
cracking the Sunday summer sky
with the hated Lullaby
　　　that now marches.
With The Lullaby that's taken 1,112 and counting
past the dawn
with The Lullaby.
The Lullaby.
The Lullaby that's left so many others like myself
single
in the street.
Until I finally found these hundreds of thousands
of solitary others
at Columbus Circle

on June 24, 1990.
And blew Larry Kramer kisses
    all the way down to the Hudson.

Hour
after hour
after hour
after hour on a beer-splashed bank
of the Christopher Street River of Pride
I tossed hundreds of SILENCE=DEATH,
Read My Lips,
Keith Haring
large, medium, small
Tee-shirts
over a cardboard box fort
to a busy, beaming man of middle age
working the booth,
spending his time,
like me
to fight The Lullaby.

"I'm going to wear this Read My Lips one for *People* magazine photos with my family," he laughed. "Because tomorrow, the 25th, is my birthday."

"Oh, happy birthday!" I said. "My birthday's on Wednesday, the 27th."

"June 27th?" he said. "You know, that is the actual date of the Stonewall Riots."

. . .

"Yeah. I know."

His eyes and teeth lit up the falling twilight
as he reached for my face.

That was the night Larry Kramer kissed me.

End of Part Three.

Owed to the Village People

Part One

(An 8-year-old boy at bedtime in his room, kneeling at stool (for bed) saying his good-night prayers. Objects he presents are mimed; probably hidden under the bed. Performer may also act out the scenarios and people he describes: séance, paperweight making, father, mother, Rudolph, Village People, being chased through the woods, etc. A child playing in his bedroom, the safest place in his world.)

Now I lay me down to sleep.
I pray the Lord my soul to keep.
If I should die before I wake,
I pray the Lord my soul to take.
God Bless Mommy and Daddy . . .

(He listens to see if he can hear his parents stirring, or close to his closed bedroom door. Then proceeds to talk to God in a friendly and familiar manner.)

You know what? Mommy and me went Christmas shopping at Golden Ring Mall tonight and I got this really cool paperweight with a purple and blue butterfly in it for Daddy.

(Produces the mimed paperweight from under the stool/bed.)

They had other ones with like different-colored air bubbles and junk, and a whole bunch of different insect ones, but this one was the best one.

It's kind of like my Science Fair project for Mr. Baumgarter's class, when I caught that butterfly and left it in my Jif jar for a whole week. That was the same jar I used to catch lightning bugs last summer with Janis Gerber.

OOOO, like the night, like the night, like the night we turned out all the lights in Janis's basement, and we put the Jif jar with all the lightning bugs inside Janis's Barbie Dream House. And then I brought my Barbie over. And with Janis's Barbie, Ken, and Skipper we had this like séance in a circle around the Dream House. It was really spooky, like *Night Gallery*.

But nothing really happened, 'cause Janis's brother Brad came down and wrecked everything. He let all the lightning bugs go and he threw my Barbie into the woods.

I think Daddy'll like this, this paperweight. 'Cause he's always at his desk working and there are so many papers on his desk that this'll really be useful. Mommy says, "It's practical. And that's a good thing to keep in mind when buying gifts."

(Imitates mother's taking a drag on cigarette.)

But whatever. I just think its supercool the way they can get a butterfly inside all that glass. They must have to like catch millions of butterflies from all over the world. And they must like have millions and millions of Jif jars. And then, when they're all dried and dead, they pin them on cork, just like I did for the Science Fair, and then they pick the prettiest ones, and then very carefully they pour boiling-hot glass on top of them in some sort of metal mold machine, and then TA-DA! . . . . Paperweights.

I'll bet that's a really great job, butterfly hunting.

(He listens again to see if parents are stirring or close to his closed bedroom door.)

And you know what else? Mommy let me go Christmas shopping by myself for a whole half an hour. I wanted to get her a bracelet, or a pin, or some earrings, or a necklace. But she never really wears them. I guess they're not really practical. But Mommy really loves music. She's always putting on those Supremes records when she's cleaning up and stuff around the house; she's always sort of singing along and dancing around to them Supremes records. So, I was going to get her a brand-new Supremes record, but the man at the record store said: "There aren't any new ones. They don't make them anymore!" But then I remembered when I got my hair cut last month at Rudolph's Unisex Hair Salon, Rudolph was playing this record on his stereo and he was kind of singing along and dancing around while he was cutting my hair—it was really cool music—and he told me they were a new band called Village People.

So I got it for Mommy for Christmas!

(Produces mimed album from under stool/bed.)

That's a useful gift.

Oh, but when I told Janis about them, after I'd heard them at Rudolph's, she said "They're fairies!" She said her brother Brad told her so, and Brad would know—Brad's in a band.

But they don't look like fairies on the record cover. They look really tough—really cool. There's a Cowboy and an Indian and a Policeman and an Army Guy and a Motorcycle Guy—and he looks really tough. And there's a Construction Guy just like the ones I saw working on Route 40 last summer.

So, why are they called Village People? Do they all like live in the same small town or something? Or maybe they all like live in the same development, like the one we live in—Edgewood Village. Maybe like that, and they all met at the pool. And that's when they all became friends! Or like in that song—the one I heard at Rudolph's—at the YMCA.

(Sings "YMCA., Hang out with boys! YMCA.")

And that's when they made a band like Brad and his band, or like at school, like Cliffy Bollman and those guys.

Like them?

Boy, if I was big and tough like the Village People, Cliffy sure wouldn't mess with me. He'd be the one getting chased through the woods, and I'd pin him down, and I'd pin him on cork, and then I'd put him inside of a paperweight. And I'd put him on my desk where I could always look at him and say: "See Cliffy! See what happens when you mess with me!"

If I was big and tough like the Village People.

(Picking up mimed paperweight and screaming at it with deep, primal rage:)

FAIRYYYYYYYYYYYYY!

End of scene.

Why I Go to the Gym

(Scene: Performer moves through various locales of an average gym/health club—front desk, locker room, workout areas—as the dialogue indicates. Performer should change out of pants and shoes—into shorts and sneakers—in locker room. (A jockstrap is worn underneath.) Stool is moved about the stage to accommodate the actions and locations. A metal pole— concealed onstage, but with easy access—is used to realize each exercise (as indicated in the actions of the text: dumbbell, barbell, lat machine, treadmill, and, in the final transformation, a rifle). One other acting note: whenever a line of dialogue is placed in quotation marks, it is something the character is actually, in reality, saying aloud. All else is an internal narration of the actions, thoughts, and attitudes spoken aloud, a la Rod Serling.)

You slap down that membership card that lets you into . . .
The Warrior Room.
Where the men dress like boys.
But it's only an outfit for the transformation:
turning the boys
. . . into men.

. . .

In The Changing Room
it's hushed with the concentrated effort of removing
all your clothes;
with or without attention paid to the size . . .
of your cock.

(Removing pants, noticing audience:)

Especially at the moment.
Amongst the other guys snapping
snaps,
belts,
and elastic straps
against their naked buttocks,
brushing your own wriggling, naked buttocks into a pair
of gray cotton Calvin Klein's.

(Pulling on shorts:)

MMMmmmm, yeah . . .
that's why I go to the gym.

(Putting on sneakers, sitting on stool:)

Take a whiff of Old Spice lockers,
    damp white towels,
    musk,
    steam,
    soap,
    cream

. . . and pubic hairs dried to the strangest places.

(Picks one off of somewhere very near him—stool, shoe, etc.—and flicks it away.)

Catching glimpses.
Or staring right out at the guys you've wanted since the
    day you
first feared the sensations they gave you in the junior high
showers. Only now . . .
you can "do it."

MMMmmmm, yeah . . .
that's why I go to the gym.

> But be warned. And beware.
> Because it's a mix of Us and Them.
> Yeah, they're here, too. Pumping up.
> Remember that.

You take a water-fountain-stroll
that gives you a chance
to check out the scene.
Hmmm, not too crowded . . . but cute.
Yeah, Trey looks pretty damn good with a salon-bought-tan
bursting over Nair'd tits and tummy.
Yeah, his bod sure did benefit from all
those winter workouts
. . . so did his T cells.
Nobody'd suspect he's sick,

not the way he flaunts that spandex-spread-dick—

(Calling out across the room, in fey voice:)

    "HEY, TREY, GREAT SHORTS!!!"
MMMmmmm, yeah . . . that's why I go to the gym.

I think I'll do some curls.

(Picking up metal pole, positioning stool to sit on.
Proceeds, using pole as dumbbell, speaking dialogue in
rhythm with exercises.)

MMMmmmm, yeah.
My biceps
look great:
re-flec-ting off of ev-ery wall
in the room.
While ev-ery-one
in the room is
watch
-ing
me
curl
and
pump
up.
Hard
blue
veins

sna-king-up-my-fore-arm
to my
bubble-
knot-
bi-
cep.
MMMmmm, yeah. That's why I go to the gym.

I think I'll do some bulking UP!

(Pole as barbell off floor.)

But first I'll
rep, rep, rep-e-ti-tion
set, set, set to-build-my
py-ra-mid
up-to-the-
high-est
weight!

Felt that burn.

MMMmmmm, yeah. That's why I go to the gym.

I think I'll push my lats—
        there's one.
        Coming towards me.
Push my lats
out-so-far-my-arms-won't-lie-a-gainst-my
nar-row-tight-slim-

hips
which-is-where-my-V-
sits
to-su-pport-my-
taut-
broad-
chipped-
kicked-
shoul-der-
spread!

(*Looking up from stool, after final lat machine pull, he sees someone. It is a straight man—"Them"—who asks to cut in.*)

"Sure. Go ahead."

(*Performer gets off stool, steps to side, and observes this "intruder" go through a set of lat pulls out of the corner of his eye. After intruder's set is completed, performer returns to do another set of lat pulls.*)

I gotta get wide,
wide,
wide-e-nough-to-hold-the-world-on.
Wide,
wide,
wide-e-nough-to-knock-the-world-down
when-they-get-too-close
to-these-taut-broad-chipped-kicked-shoulder-spread!

The Night Larry Kramer Kissed Me   37

(He rises and goes to leave, when he is approached by the "intruder" again—to assist him on his next lat set.)

"Yeah, I'll spot you."

(Performer stands behind stool, with pole in hands out in front of him, as if spotting.)

Keep pull-ing-down-down-down
with-a-grip-grip-grip
tight-e-nough-to-take-the-trip-when-I-get-kicked
down-down-down-to-the-ground-ground-ground
by-the-shoul-ders-who-are-knock-ing-me-down
on-my-street,
arm-to-arm-in-packs-that-roam-my-street
roam-my-street
roam-my-street
hun-ting-down-my-kind-of-meat.

(Performer finishes the spotting, goes to move away, carrying pole.)

That's why I go to the . . . "No. It's all yours. Knock yourself out!"

CRUNCHES!

To-rip-ple-my-sto-mach-to-wash-board-en-dur-ance
(breath-breath-breath)—
yeah,

that's-why-I-go-to-the-gym.
To-ge-ge-get-hard
ge-ge-get-cold
ge-ge-get-numb
a-a-and-I-won't-have-to-fell-
the-pun-che-che-ches-
of-the-straight-o-ppre-e-e-ssors!
(breath-breath-breath)
yeah,
that's why I go to the gym.

*(Performer walks treadmill in place, using pole as a
balancing beam handle. The pole's identity changes
towards the end of this final section as the performer's
slow treadmill gait picks up to an in-place jog,
handling the pole as a rifle as the rhythms of the
dialogue break into military marching cadences.)*

To-tigh-ten-up-my-ass.
To-please-the-lov-er-I-don't-have-so-I-can-get-one
to-fuck-one
with-a-con-dom
to-pro-tect-one
from-the-stalk-ing
that-is-go-ing
down-on-my-street
a-ttack-ing-dykes-&-fag-gots-who-are-dy-ing
as-they're-ly-ing-down-on-my-street
Yeah
That's-Why-I-Go-To-The-Gym!

(Tempo of jog picks up, along with the pace of the dialogue.)

So-my-pec-tor-als-get-pinched-more
my-nip-ples-they-get-pinched-more
and-my-chest-gets-tight-like-an-armor-plate
a-vest-of-steel
an-armor-plate
so-I'll-be-pre-pared-to-meet
kil-lers-out-there-wait-ing-for
the-fag-gots-like-the-ones-I-love
who-pump-up-here-be-side-me-for
the-day-when-they-come-'round-for-us
to-kick-us
and-to-kill-us.
Queers-who've-got-ten-jabbed-be-fore.

(Jog-2-3-4.)

Ta-ken-lots-of-stabs-be-fore.

(Jog-2-3.)

-Be-fore-the-day-we-joined-the-gym-to-meet
the-le-vel-of-the-ha-tred.

(Breaks into military drill cadences, pole swings into rifle position, jogging continues at same even tempo.)

We're-to-build-our-selves-for-hands-on-war

our-bo-dies-are-our-weap-ons-for
the-day-we-bash-the-bash-ers-back
in-to-the-graves-they've-dug-for-us
so-we-can-have-the-fin-al-laugh
when-we-sit-back-&-tell-the-lore
of-how-we-won-the-final-war

*(Jog switches into an even march in four silent beats
without dialogue.)*

When-we-be-gan-the-pump-ing
and-the-pull-ing
and-the-curl-ing
and-the-cut-ting
and-the-lunging-and-the-repping-and-the-crunching-
and-the-pressing-towards-the-day-we-win-the-
FI-
NAL-
WAR-
FROM-
GO-
ING-
TO-

THE GYM.

End of scene.

12″ Single

(Scene: Performer preparing at home in front of a full-length mirror—the final adjustments of dressing—for a late night club crawl, the search for love. As in Why I Go to the Gym, *the majority of the dialogue is an internal narration of the actions, thoughts, and attitudes of the character's journey: the stream-of-consciousness spoken aloud as he travels and chronicles each location indicated in the text. And also as before, dialogue in quotation marks indicates the character's* real-life *responses. This scene is set to a recorded composition, arranged and recorded by Steven Sandberg. It has roots in rap, for sure, but is not to be considered a musical number. The actual music drives and steadies the scene—with musical highlights responding to the spoken dialogue—serving as a foundation for the character's trip.)*

Girth is everything.
Inches count.
6 inches
by 6 inches
equals 12 inches
equal me:
Single.
GWM: 29, 5′9, 150 lbs.,
blond-slash-blue.

A 12-inch single, smart, smooth, swimmer seeks . . .
you.

And you.
And you.
And you.
And you and you and you and you
And you and you and you and you hit the streets at 1 A.M.,
smellin' sweet, Yves Saint Laurent.

Leather jacket,
Tee-shirt pressed,
501's and boots,
we're set . . .

for walkin'.

Boots
were made
for walkin'.

Walkin', walkin', walkin', walkin'
on the streets at 1 A.M.
to the cell
where they keep the men.

A holding pen.

Enter.
I'm smellin' smoke,

smellin' piss,
smellin' coke,
smellin' jis-
    "... um, yeah. Give me a Rolling Rock."
Boys & boys & boys & boys.
I'm lookin', lookin', lookin', lookin'.
All I need is love & you & music, music, music-
    "Thanks!"

(Drinks entire beer he has ordered in one gulp.)

Casual Consumption.

Single, single, single, single
single boys all around.
In every crook.
In every crack.
In every
single
square
inch.
Hit the floor.
There's room for more.
Hit it hard.
Hit on me.
Shake your bootie.
Twist & Quake/
    "Hey, easy, boy! Don't break your shake."
    'Cause you will bake
later.

. . .

Casual consumption
of
all
these
boys & boys & boys & boys.
I'm lookin', lookin', lookin', lookin'.
All I need is love & you & music, music, music.
Music.
Music.
Music.
Music.
Music, music.
Music, music, music, music,
music, music, music, music!
Play it loud.
Play it fast.
Play it, play it, play it, play it,
play it, play it, play it, play it
loud enough
and fast enough
to shock me.
Fill me.
Take me.
Hit me.
Hit me.
Hit me.
Hit me.
Hit me, hit me, hit me, hit me
HIT

ON
ME.
You there, Mr. Care Bear!

Don't let HIV slow you down.
 Upbeat & Positive:
   GWM, 38, 5'10", 195 lbs.,
   brown-slash-brown,
   muscle butch top with hair,
   hair,
   hair, hair, hair, hair, hair, hair, hair, hair, HAIR.
   Sense of humor.
 Seeks: slim, trim, cleancut, clean-shaven
    dancer-bod for
    cock-sucking,
    butt-working,
    tit-clamping,
    and TLC.

    . . . Redheads a Plus!

So many men.
So little time
and taste.

I'm a 12 Inch Single:
play me once, flip me over, play me twice.
Hit me.

Boys & boys & boys & boys.

The Night Larry Kramer Kissed Me 47

I'm lookin', lookin', lookin', lookin'.
All I need is love and you and music, music, music,
cute.
He's cute.
And cuddly.

> *Cute & Cuddly:*
>> GWM, 32, 5′2″, 120 lbs.,
>> Dewy drop eyes.
>> Generous, concerned, and CLEAN.
>> *Lookin' for:* good-hearted, AIDS-negative,
>>> regular-guy for
>>> friendship,
>>> fun times,
>>> and fist fucks!

>> Rubber glove it good.

>> Your Dick gets mine
>> . . . plus MORE.

Hit me, hit me, hit me, hit me,
Hit
on
me, oh knocked out by your love.
Boys & boys & boys & boys.
I'm lookin', lookin', lookin', lookin'.
All I need is love and you and music, music, music,
You: Clark
Kent.

Me: Jimmy
Olsen.

Gladiator Guppie:
    GWM, 25, 6′5″, 250 lbs.,
    blond-slash-green.
    Nine-to-five broker by day,
    Master of Your Universe by Night!
    Demands: spanking-whipping-boy-slave,
        18-dash-21
        for light S&M FUN.
    Get beneath my Brooks Brothers and then
    GET ON YOUR KNEES!
        No fats.
    No fems.
        No.
    No.
        No.
    No.

    Just Say No.
    Hit me.

Boys & boys & boys & boys.
I'm lookin', lookin', lookin', lookin'.
All I need is love and you and music, music, music.
I'm a 12 Inch Single.
Play me once, flip me over, play me twice.

I am to lead

a glamorous life.
I only need
a man's PUNCH.
Hit me, hit me, hit me, hit me.
Hit
on
Hello, Mr. Speedo. Volleyball anyone?
Hey, my court's free!

     GWM, 22, 6′2″, 180 lbs.,
     blond-slash-blue.
     Gym Built,
     Ivy League,
     Suc-cessful Pro-fessional.
     Seeks SAME:
          for
          water sports on rubber sheets.

Straight-Acting, Straight-Appearing ONLY
          need
          apply.

     Oh, yeah.
     Straight-Acting, Straight-Appearing ONLY
     need
     apply.

No chubs.
     No ugs.
And no, no, no ballerinas PLEASE!

David Drake   50

Boys & boys & boys & boys.

I'm lookin', lookin', lookin', lookin'.

All I need is love and you and music, music, music.

I'm a 12 Inch Single:

Play me once, flip me over, play me twice!

Yo, Arsenio! I see "The Myth" is true!

> GBM, 31, 6'1", 191 lbs.
>
> Very Masculine.
>
> Up-
>
> up-
>
> up-
>
> up-wardly mobile
>
> likes skiing, sailing, saunas
>
> *Seeks Roommate:*
>
> > for Straight-Acting, Straight-Appearing,
> >
> > White-Acting, White-Appearing
> >
> > Re-
> >
> > la-
> >
> > tion-
> >
> > ship.
> >
> > Repeat: Straight-Acting, Straight-Appearing,
> >
> > White-Acting, White-Appearing
> >
> > Re-
> >
> > la-
> >
> > tion-
> >
> > ship.

Shit.

Boys & boys & boys & boys.

I'm lookin', lookin', lookin', lookin'.
All I need is love and you . . .

(Performer mimes snorting poppers, or coke, found in jacket pocket.)

and you . . .

(Spotting someone across the room—most effectively played with that someone at the back of the theater, facing the audience.)

you.
You, you, you, you 12 Inch Single
with your back to my face.
Watchin' all us go-go boys
twist in place
to the beat
of our meat.
Pounding for who?

For You?

Yeah, you.
You.
You, you, you, you beer-slick lips,
and ice-blue eyes
starin' at me.
You hear my cries?

• • •

Hey, soldier . . . what's your size?

See, I'm a 12 Inch Single
you can play me once.
Baby, you can throw me over and soldier boy . . . ?
You can play me twice.
Take it.
Take it out.
Take it out on me.
Yeah, you,
ice-blue.
Yeah, cruise me.
Choose me.
Abuse me.
Lose me.
Boy, tie me up.
Boy, tie me down.
Boy . . .

. . . hey.
Hey.
Hey, Soldier!
Hey, don't divert your eyes from me.
Hey, look here
QUEEEEEEEEEEEEEEEEEERRRRRRRRRRRRRR!
Well, maybe you're a little too light,
faggot.

Homo.

• • •

Boy-Girl.

Ballerina.
Mama's Boooyyyyy!
Pansy-sissy-nelly-wussy-
fem-fruit-queen-freak-
girly-missy-mary-fairy-
cock-suckin', mother-fuckin' chicken.

CHICKEN!

Are you chicken, soldier-chicky?

Chicken-chicken-chicken-chicken-
chicken-chicken-chicken-
YO! DOG-BITCH, BOY-PUSSY,
PILLOW-CHOMPIN' BOTTOM!
I'M TALKIN' TO YOU!

HEY, HOMO-CUNT!

(Performer pulls hunting knife from his pocket. It is not produced as a weapon, but rather as an abstract symbol of violence.)

I got your 12 Inch Single
I will play you once.
Homo, I will kick you over
and soldier-sissy
I will fuck you twice
as hard.

(Performer begins to move knife over his body.)

Boy, oh boy, oh boy, oh boy, oh boy, oh boy, oh yeah
I see you lookin', lookin', lookin', lookin'.
lookin', lookin', lookin', lookin'.
All I need
is you to
hit
on
me.

And music.
Music.
Music,
music,
music,
music,
music-music
music, music, music, music, music, music, music, music,

MMMMMM-
you-
sick . . .
yeah.

MMMMMMMMM-
you-
sick . . .
yeah.

. . .

MMMMMMMMMMMMMM-
Yooooooooouuuuuuu-
Sick.

MMMMMMMMMMMMMMMMMMMM-
YOOOOOOOOOOOUUUUUUUUUUU-
SICK.

MMMMMMMMMMMMMMMMMMMMMMMMMMMM
YOOOOOOOOOOOOOOOOUUUUUUUUUUUUUUUUU
SICK.

. . . "Let's go."

End of scene.

Owed to the
Village People

Part Two

Now I lay me down to sleep.
I pray the Lord my soul to keep.
If I should die before I wake,
I pray the Lord my soul to take.
God bless Mommy and Daddy, and Grandma and
Grandpap, Uncle Jim and Aunt Barb, and Janice,
and Smokey, and Misty.

And God?
Bless the Village People.

End of scene.

A Thousand Points of Light

(Scene: Nightime. A candlelight vigil on a New York City street. Performer lights a single candle at the top of the scene, before any dialogue is spoken, and carries it throughout.)

I've got this.
I've got this light.
I've got this one point of light to steer me, guide me
    through the night.
With a thousand points of light that now surround me,
    engulf me
    here on the street.
We vigil.
    We meet.
        We carry The Dead.

In a moment of stillness,
in a moment of semblance,
in a moment
of silence
we search
in the night,
with the night,
through the night that's hiding those who went.

So be careful when you blink,
>   or think
>   that's it,
>   no more,
>   I can't absorb another memory,
> >   'cause someone else is missing.

>   Where did you go?

Andy?
Bobby?
Danny?
Frank?
Gary?
>   Gary?

> > Gary, you were the first. A neighbor, right next
> > door. I could tell you were sick the moment I met
> > you, the night I moved into the building. But you
> > never brought it up. And I didn't want to know
> > about it, I didn't want to start. But you kept
> > showing up at my door, bringing me "things,"
> > which started with: "I hate to bother you, but I
> > was just cleaning up and I came across this little
> > leather baseball cap I thought would look real
> > cute on you. Would you like it?"

Sure.

A Key West beach towel.
A wicker picnic basket.

A box of Gordon Merrick paperbacks.

And tapes, tapes, all those tapes which started with:

> "I hate to bother you, but these walls are so thin, and God knows I love music—it's my life—and your Dionne Warwick's . . . very nice. But I just think you ought to try some Bette. Here she is, *Live at Last— in Cleveland!*

I only came to visit at the hospital that night because you called and asked for your mail:

> "I hate to bother you, but I'm expecting the *Divine Madness* sound track from Columbia House."

I was just going to breeze through with "Hi, here's your tape, how are you, bye," as I entered into the ward, and into your room, and into you hacking your lungs out, and into that big black man at the foot of your bed, screaming into the nurse's face:

> "Get me the bedpan. Get me the bedpan. Get me the bedpan. Get me the bedpan. GET ME THE BED- PAAAANNN!"

It was like Shirley MacLaine playing *Terms of Endearment* a hundred and seventeen times better.

That nurse flew out of the room, arms stretched, as that big black man stepped into my face and said:

> "You the neighbor?"

I said, "Yeah."

He said,

"Good."
He said,

> "Why don't you do the neighborly thing
> and find me some clean, dry sheets. 'Cause these ones
> here . . . they're soakin' with shit."

> Exit: Harlow.
> The Ex-Lover.

We took you home at the end of that week, I think. Yeah:

> "I hate to bother you."

And then back. And then home. And back and home and back and home and sometimes, Gary, when you were at home, late at night, I'd turn out all the lights in my apartment and press my ear to the wall to hear you puttering around singing softly to those records . . .

(Recalls this memory by gently singing opening stanza of Bette Midler's "Skylark.")

Asleep?
Just checking.
All safe.
And then I could go to sleep.

That knock at the door I was sure was you, but it was Harlow with his arms full of shoeboxes:

> "Gary was just cleaning up and he wants you to have
> these. But, come on, let's get out of here . . . I'm
> starved."

So we took a stroll down into the Village for something to eat at the Tiffany Diner. Harlow said:

>"Breakfast at Tiffany's! I know exactly what we'll eat. My treat!"

And Harlow ordered,

>"Pancakes & Beer!!!"

Breakfast at Tiffany's.
Harlow's idea.
Yum.

>"Listen, those shoeboxes are full of Gary's tapes. But if you don't like any of them, please don't throw them out—just pass them on."

When we returned
it was so quiet.
In a moment of stillness.
No "Skylark."
Asleep?

You were gone.

Where did you go?

But Gary? The night wasn't over—for not a moment had passed with you in it that Harlow, *you* were sick. And so I just picked up where you had just left off; doing twice the things in half the time. I was moving so fast, moving so fast and, still, Harlow, all you kept saying was:

>"Come on, baby. Come on, baby. Come on, baby. Come

on, baby. 'Cause I got an appointment. I got an appointment. I got an appointment. I GOT AN APPOINTMENT TO KEEP!!!"

And you must've,
In a moment of semblance
'cause in a month
and a week
you left.

Where did you go, Harlow?

Jose?
Kenny?
Meghan?
Paul?

 Paul?

  Paul, you singing-dancing-New Age-"Let Go"-gypsy-chorus-boy-queen. God, I loved you.

  And, boy, I should've known you'd leap to tour when I suggested that maybe our dating was moving toward a relationship. "Oh, no, no, no, no, no," you said, "I have a career!"

  "You've got to let go, let go, let go," you said, " 'cause *God, I'm a dancer and a dancer dances!*' "

You people-pleasing prick tease.

But who kept calling
from those midnight motel rooms on the road?
You. Not me.

You,

who closed in Phoenix and called me at 3 A.M. saying:

    "Help. What do I do?"

Come here, Paul. Come home.

    "OK, OK, OK," you said. "But before New York,

    I've got to see my family

    soon."

Two months passed, Paul. Two.

Where the hell did you go?

Except for that picture postcard of the St. Louis Airport

   that said:

    "Soon. Paul."

I didn't hear a goddamned thing from you.

Soon.

Soon.

Yeah, soon the phone rang.

It was Tanya in Harrisburg, PA,

your sister, saying:

    "You're the friend? You'd better come . . .

    soon."

I was so fucking mad at you, Paul, I waited a week before I got on that train for Harrisburg. You'd bounced around the country for the past 11 months in those two-horse towns for those dead-beat hicks who'd never heard of HIV, never gave a flying fuck about that beautiful young man kicking & belting his guts out up there on that stage to win their approval, win their attention, win their praise without a heartbeat of a glimmer of a pause of a thought that that beautiful young man's blood coursed with a poison that was

drilling his life away every second up there on that goddamned stage. Those selfish fucking bastards and their
selfish fucking "Taste" for fucking "Escape." "ESCAPE!"
What do they need to "Escape" FROM?! Oh, God, to this
minute I still hate musicals.

And fuck you, Paul. Fuck you. 'Cause every fucking time I
even mentioned seeing a doctor, blood work, T cells,
counts, ANYTHING, you shooed me away with that
    "giving into the negative,"
    "giving into the dis-ease" bullshit.
You had so much energy, Paul.
Where did it go?

Soon.

Harrisburg.

In that night,
in that room,
holding your hand
I sat by your side,
and though our hands held
contained,
baby, *you* did not.
Rather you seemed all over the room
wandering
        —gently, cautiously—
In a moment
        —suddenly, quietly—

of silence
you got away.

Where did you go?

I went through the weekend, and the family, and the food,
and the flowers, and the phone calls, and the viewing,
and the viewing, and the viewing, and the viewing,
and don't Catholics believe in cremation, what?

And the neighbors.
And the Priest.
And your mother's introduction: "Paul's Friend."
And Tanya's insistence: "Paul's LOVER."

And the whispers.
You would've been furious.
And the stares.
But I loved it. Let go. I did.
And the limo.
What did you tell her, Paul—I was your lover?
And the lowering.
Why?
And the dirt.

Is that how you told me?

We carry the dead.

Tanya called last Christmas—she's pregnant.

The Night Larry Kramer Kissed Me   69

Baby's expected to arrive
    soon.

Terry?
Vito?
Will?
    Will?
          Will, where was I going that night?
          Oh, right—to meet the boys of bereavement group
          for coffee at the diner.
          But I didn't have a dime
          and so I stood in line
          at the bank machine
          watching a baseball-capped, ACT UP Warrior
          wheatpaste posters onto the building
          I was about to take money from,
          who smiled at me and came right up to me
          and said: "Haven't we met?"
          I said no.
          You said,
               "Yeah." You said, "Didn't we get arrested
               at Saint Patrick's together?"
          I said no, I've never even been arrested.
          You said,
               "Oh. Welllllll, what're you doing tonight?"

Nothing.

And so I followed you into that night—
    into a City Hall demo;

budget cuts, needle exchange, condoms . . . ?
I don't believe I don't remember that now,
'cause I was completely swept up into that night
and into the hurricane of clarity,
of organization of grieving,
of anger
equals action
equals life
equals people
equals meetings and dittos
and Treatment and Data
and posters and stickers and speeches
and "Point of Order,"
steering committees,
working groups,
civil disobedience training
and chanting and handcuffs
and court orders and service
and sit-ins and kiss-ins and die-ins and zaps
and The Night.
Equals *"The Night We Took Back the Street"!*

Equals the night
    we took back

        on your bed.

It was the night
   we went to see Ethyl Eichelberger!
ETHYL!

In that show of his own solo creation:
of smoke and mirrors
and mascara and stilettos
and fire and music
and rhinestones and mischief and magic
Ethyl Magic.
Who cast a spell upon our eyes
and ears and hands and hearts.
Into our night,
        into our core

                into queer.

Which sent us skipping through the East Village
    streets
        wailing songs of *Strong Women,*
        all the way into a queer-cave-club
        to twist and flick a slick of sweat
        onto the dance floor's blackened cement.
        And before the world called it day,
        we fled to your fifth-floor-walk-up-flight
        to take and squeeze what little was left
        of our night
        in with each other,
                inside each other

                tight.

        And as the sun cut a venetian-blind-slice
        across my face and into our night

you covered my eyes with your hands
and inhaling my whispered breath, you said:
"We're past the sex."
"We're past the moment of one."
"We're Brother to Brother."
     And we slept
        Brother to Brother.

In a moment of stillness
    Where did you go?
In a moment of semblance
    You still in San Francisco?
In a moment
    Will?
of silence
     Brother?

      Or are you with Ethyl now?

      Ethyl.

Where did you go?

You doing a show? Somewhere? Starring in a show tonight?
A solo star show.
A star.

*(In this last attempt to make spiritual sense of this
loss—the loss of hope, for Ethyl Eichelberger committed
suicide after the AIDS drug AZT failed him—*

The Night Larry Kramer Kissed Me   **73**

Performer's search leads him to the night sky, locating a star.)

There you are.

I've got this.
I've got this light.
I've got this one point of light to steer me, guide me
     through the night.
Toward a thousand points of light that now surround me,
     engulf me
     here on the street.
We vigil.
     We meet
          in the night,
               with the night,
                    as the night that hovers with those
                         who went.

               And they carry us, our dead.

And so be careful when you blink,
     or think:
     that's it.
     No more.
     I can't absorb another memory
     'cause someone else is missing.
I know where you went.
We're all here in the night.

Even you, little one, off to the right.
Have I seen you?
Have we ever met?
        "Twinkle, twinkle, little star.
        How I wonder who you are."
I know you.
        You never-famous
                never-counted
                never-quoted
                never-seen
                Nobody
                Somebody's Best Little Boy in the World.
        Who came here to the city from some town
        some small town
        maybe Youngstown, Ohio
        searching for "Somewhere"
                for yourself
                maybe for me?
        Like all of us to find yourself searching in the
            night.
        Maybe we even passed each other on the street
                but it's so hard to see in the night.
        Maybe you were out of my sight when you
            passed
                through the night.

        Maybe I never heard you
                singing softly to your records
                        but my ear still listens.

Maybe we never shared a "Breakfast at Tiffany's"
　　　of pancakes & beer
　　　　　but they're still serving and I'll treat.
Maybe I wasn't the one you called
　　　at 3 A.M. asking for help, soon
　　　　　but my phone still alarms
　　　　　in the middle of the night
　　　　　and I awaken and I answer.
Maybe I never pulled you onto the front lines
　　　and we never got arrested together
　　　　　but I'm still fighting.
And maybe we never took each other on a bed
　　　Brother to Brother.
But my eyes are still triggered to my heart
　　　and to my flesh
　　　to lend warmth
　　　to the Brothers
　　　left here
　　　left queer
　　　left together
　　　in the night.

　　　And so I know you.
　　　I honor you.
　　　I love you.
　　　I light this light for you.

　　　For somewhere
　　　　　　　•　•　•

in a moment of stillness

in a moment of semblance

in a moment

(Here, the actual Moment of Silence—a tribal, meditative remembrance of the dead, customary in candlelight vigils and Gay Pride Day celebrations—is engaged instead of saying the words "in silence.")

. . . we'll meet.

End of scene.

"... and *The Way We Were*"

(Scene: New Year's Eve, 1999—about ten minutes before midnight. Performer begins scene offstage, with dialogue being directed to his lover.)

She can too still sing!

(Performer sings opening line of the title song from the movie The Way We Were. *His singing stops in a burst of giggles—as if he is being seduced and/or tickled very playfully by his lover, fending the lover off with protests of:)*

OK, stop it, Button. OK, OK, OK, just get the glasses, would you?

(Performer enters onstage and addresses the audience very casually—breaking the fourth wall—as if he is simply telling some stories to the guests gathered in his home.)

He is so frisky tonight. Must've been the movie. We just saw the remake of that Redford/Streisand classic *The Way We Were* starring Tom Cruise and Jason Streisand, uh,

GOULD. So romantic! And Jason is really moving, really fierce in Barbra's old role as the activist. What, Button?

(Responding to offstage comments from lover.)

Oh, come on! Barbra's got to get the Directing Oscar this time!!! Yes, the glasses are in the freezer.

(Back, talking to audience:)

Oh, the movie made tonight just right, because not only does the stroke of midnight mark the start of the twenty-first century, it also marks the one-year anniversary of my Legal Domestic Partnership with Button . . . uh, Bill.
Oh, God, we had this crazy "Celebration Weekend" with our families and all. My folks were fine, but Bill's were ridiculous . . . with a photo session, and all this preparation fuss surrounding the Celebration Party at the Queer Pier Dance Hall on Lake Erie. Buffalo—that's where Bill's family lives. I guess in some ways it was still kind of "Old World," but all our friends who flew in thought it was pretty great.
I think my father's worn out his video of it. Or at least he's worn out the whole damn county. He shows it to anyone who asks, "Hey, how's your newlywed son doin'?"
     Oh, Dad.
What, Button? *(Responding to offstage lover.)*
Five minutes? OK, I'll be in, hon.
WHAT?
Oh, stop it. Well, I thought the re-creation of the '96 *Pentagon Action* was very true, very REAL.

(Comments to audience:) Bill got his earlobe shot off in that one.

(Calling to Bill, lamely:) My hero.

(Back to audience:)

I nearly lost him . . . yeah, and myself. But we lived.

I don't know how.

Why?

Five minutes. In five minutes we leave this twentieth century for the next and with us a whole lot of wounds; some healed, a lot not. And a whole lot of brothers and sisters dead from The Plague. And then, from the fighting—inspired in the spirit of Rosa Parks, passed on to us queer folks through you . . .

you . . .

you . . .

You, drag queens smashing down the invisible Stonewall! You're pioneering the frontier for all of us crashing out of The Closet and into the streets; paving our way through The Advocate Years with "Gay is Good," Heritage of Pride, the Gay Activists Alliance, Harvey Milk, Sylvester, and sex that flows like Niagara.

But here comes The Plague and we're crying like Niagara as we shovel dirt onto everyone we know—Rock Hudson, The Quilt, David Summers, Keith Haring, Silence=Death. Our eyes are dry, crisp with anger, and we're smashing invisible, fearful, hateful walls again—ACT UP, Fight Back, Fight AIDS.

(Pondering that distant, familiar street chant, quietly:)

ACT UP. . . . Fight Back. . . . Fight AIDS.

(Breaking into the triumphantly full-throated street demo soldier chant:)

ACT UP! FIGHT BACK! FIGHT AIDS!
ACT UP! FIGHT BACK! FIGHT AIDS!
'CAUSE WE ACT UP KIDS ARE OUT TO SAVE OUR
    EVERY BREATH!!

Then ACT UP joined NOW, WHAM!, WAC, TAG, the NAACP, GMHC, HRCF, the ACLU, NGLTF, PWAC, PFLAG, the AFL-CIO, the ya-da-da, ya-da-da-da-da-da . . . and we made our demands. Urvashi and Tom Duane, and Jesse Jackson and Barbara Jordan joined hands with Barbara Boxer and Gerry Studds, and Marlo and Phil, and Magic, and Whoopi . . . and the Carters: Jimmy, Rosalynn, and Amy—with her lover . . . Chastity!

For the *Together We'll Take Manhattan Action.*

It was five days into the blackout that The Cure was released. And they'd had it. No, they'd had it for almost a year, but said: "The business was too good to stop since cancer had grown passé." That's a quote—Louis Sullivan.

And nobody gets a Nobel. Shame. Shame. The shame was too great.

Gallo, Schlafly, Dannemeyer . . . oh, a lot of them are in prison now. Anthony Fauci disappeared. Poof! We think he's in South America. That's where they found Ed Koch.

Yes, the blood certainly was on their hands, but in the Queer War of '96, it was also dripping off our own, from our own. '96 . . . oh, the year we lost Mr. Kramer. Which really sobered us, after the delight from the Rush Limbaugh assassination.

Enjoy that while it lasts!

But get prepared, Chicago, San Francisco, L.A., Dallas, Atlanta, D.C., Boston, New York . . . 'cause the blood and fire will tear through your cities . . .

Oh, God . . . Chuck. And Ed. I still miss you. But you shot right out there into the National Guard lines and I couldn't stop you. I couldn't stop the anger that took your lives, or any of the lives so many of you will give in the name of your rights.

Chuck, the monument goes up next spring in Dupont Circle that kicks off the new National Holiday. And Ed, I read on the front page of *The New York Times* today that by 2007 the Queer Cultures Wing will be completed on the Smithsonian.

Yeah, get prepared. It won't be pretty, but it's good here.

It's better. You'll see.

And you'll see . . . Joe Steffan win his suit against the Annapolis Naval Academy in the Maryland State Court of Appeals. You'll see the new Census Report, with the "Sexual Orientation" column. The results of which you'll see Kinsey's 10% was a naively low estimation. You'll see the outing of Siskel & Ebert. And a whole lot of soap stars and TV anchor people that nobody really cared about anyway. You'll see them replaced, though, by out dykes and fags, 'cause you'll see GLAAD finally gain power at the networks and MTV. Oh, and you'll see the new Madonna video!—with her safer sex seduction of an Asian woman. She's got this big Kabuki fan that spins into a dental dam!
It's FABULOUS!

(Responding to offstage lover:)

What, Button? THE COUNTDOWN!!!
Okay, I'm coming.

(Back, talking to audience:)

And you'll see people like Bill and me—out, together, walking hand in hand down the streets of New York . . . Toledo . . . Portland, Richmond, Raleigh, Tallahassee, Albuquerque, New Mexico; Morgantown, West Virginia; Pomona . . . without condemnation, restrictions, compromises, or closets. But with the freedom to love that we got . . . when we took.

You know, the truth will set you free. But first, it will piss you off. You've just got to make it here, if you want to see *The Way We Were.* Happy New Year.

("Auld Lang Syne" swells as stage lights fade to black.)

End of scene.

The End of *The Night Larry Kramer Kissed Me*

"The Night Larry Kramer Kissed Me"

opened on June 22, 1992, at the Perry Street Theatre in New York City, where it was performed by its author David Drake until March 14, 1993. Eric Paeper took over the role on March 17, 1993, and continued the run of the play until its closing on June 27, 1993.

The Off-Broadway production was produced by Sean Strub, in association with Tom Viola; directed by Chuck Brown; set design by James Morgan; lighting design by Tim Hunter; sound design by Raymond Schilke; original music for *12" Single* by Steven Sandberg; production stage manager, Ali Sherwin; assistant director, Jon Winkelman; press representative, Susanne Tighe/Boneau Bryan-Brown; company manager, Adele Bove.

The play was subsequently presented by Sean Strub in association with Stuart Berger at Life on the Water Theatre in San Francisco, where it opened April 1, 1993, and the Tiffany Theatre in Los Angeles, where it opened May 21, 1993. Mr. Drake again starred, and the production team was the same.

About the Authors

David Drake

was born on June 27, 1963, in Waynesburg, Pennsylvania. He grew up in Harford County, Maryland, the only child of two public school teachers. He began performing in local stage productions at age ten. At twenty he moved to New York City to further pursue his acting career, which led to such Off Broadway appearances as playing the title role in the Mabou Mines production of Greg Mehrten's *Pretty Boy*; originating the character/contestant "Miss Deep South" in *Pageant*; and succeeding Charles Busch in *Vampire Lesbians of Sodom*. Television appearances have included *Law & Order*; *In the Life*; *Day One*; and dozens of talk shows, including *Joan Rivers* and *Donahue*. For film, David has taken roles in *Longtime Companion*; *Naked in New York*; *It's Pat!*; and Jonathan Demme's *Philadelphia*. In 1993 David won a Village Voice OBIE Award for his performance in *The Night Larry Kramer Kissed Me*. He is currently writing a new one-actor play.

Michelangelo Signorile

is the author of *Queer in America: Sex, the Media, and the Closets of Power*. He is a contributing writer for *Out* magazine, and has also written for the *New York Times*, *The Advocate*, *The Village Voice*, *USA Today*, the *New York Post*, the *New York Daily News*, *People*, and *The Face*. A graduate of the S. I. Newhouse School of Public Communications at Syracuse University, he lives in New York City.

Author's Note

The history of a people is valuable to the population at large, but it is invaluable to those to whom this history inherently belongs. In hearing their stories, we begin to understand the experience, strength, and hope that have distinguished a people's shape, depth, and direction. These stories, if told truthfully, also hold answers and knowledge that can serve as guideposts for the future.

The history of gay men and lesbian women is a very long and diverse story of a people. *The Night Larry Kramer Kissed Me* in no way encompasses this vastness. It does, however, hold within its text historical information specific to the modern gay and lesbian community. (I say "modern" because that is how this chapter of our history has come to be defined, since June 27, 1969, the night the Stonewall Riots began. This event is now commemorated every year in cities around the world as Lesbian and Gay Pride Day.)

For this reason, I would like to offer identifications of some of the people, places, and organizations mentioned in this play that may not be commonly known in the collective culture. Because—as the New York–based artists' collective Gran Fury so distinctly put it in their graphic design contribution to the AIDS Coalition To Unleash Power—Silence = Death.

David Drake

The People

Larry Kramer—Playwright: *The Normal Heart, Sissies' Scrapbook, Just Say No, The Destiny of Me*. Novelist: *Faggots*. Screenwriter: *Women in Love*. Larry Kramer is a founding member of the first AIDS health service organization in the world, the Gay Men's Health Crisis (GMHC) in New York City, as well as being the founding father of the direct-action group the AIDS Coalition To Unleash Power (ACT-UP). His collection of essays, *Reports from the Holocaust: The Making of an AIDS Activist*, is an essential chronicle of the first decade of the epidemic.

David Summers—A popular cabaret singer throughout the 1970s. He made his New York stage debut in the groundbreakingly successful musical *The Faggot*, in which he sang a song called "New Boy in Town," which would forever be identified with his "all-American" looks and public image. Originally from Texas, David Summers was diagnosed with AIDS in the early years of the epidemic and became a ferocious activist for AIDS sufferers long before ACT-UP. A founding member of the People With AIDS Coalition (P-WAC), he holds the distinction of being the first person ever arrested in the name of AIDS activism.

Joe Steffan—The midshipman kicked out of the United States Naval Academy in 1987 for declaring he was a gay man. He chronicles his experiences in the book *Honor Bound*.

Urvashi Vaid—The former Executive Director of the National Gay and Lesbian Task Force (NGLTF), the oldest and largest political lobbying and education group for gay and lesbian civil rights in this country.

Ethyl Eichelberger—A playwright and performer as adept with the classical fare of the Trinity Repertory Company in Providence, Rhode Island, as he was with Charles Ludlam's Ridiculous Theater Company in New York City throughout the 1970s and '80s. He was very tall and very bald, and famous for twisting not only the text of classical literature but its gender identity as well (e.g., he once performed *all* the roles in a half-hour presentation of *King Lear* on the tiny stage of the Pyramid Club, a bar at Seventh Street and Avenue A in New York's East Village). In short: a Cockette-style drag queen bent on the Bard. Ethyl Eichelberger committed suicide in the summer of 1990 after the AIDS drug AZT failed to produce positive results in his treatment.

Anthony Fauci—Director of the National Institute of Allergy and Infectious Diseases.

Louis Sullivan—Former Secretary of Health and Human Services under President George Bush.

Barbara Boxer—Elected U.S. Senator from California in 1992.

Robert Gallo—Famed American scientist who claimed to have discovered the viral cause of acquired immune deficiency syndrome in HIV. In 1992, he was found to have committed scientific misconduct by lying in his official "findings" reports (having stolen and manipulated scientific information he had been "sharing" with scientists at the Pasteur Institute in France).

Phyllis Schlafly—The Anita Bryant of the 1980s. A staunch advocate in the pro-life movement, as well as of the "traditional family values" platform at the forefront of the Republican Party's agenda. Interestingly enough, her middle-aged son John (who still lives at home with Phyllis) was outed as a gay man in 1992. John has since come to her defense on this issue of his being gay, but she hasn't come to his.

William Dannemeyer—A conservative Republican U.S. Representative from California who held Kimberly Bergalis's hand throughout her testimony to Congress. An advocate for "traditional family values," he has been instrumental in the fight to do away with confidential and anonymous HIV testing, and in perpetuating the idea that there are sufferers of AIDS who are "innocent" and those who are not.

The Organizations:

NOW—National Organization for Women
WHAM—Women's Health Action and Mobilization
WAC—Women's Action Coalition

TAG—Treatment Action Group

HRCF—Human Rights Campaign Fund

P-FLAG—Parents and Friends of Lesbians and Gays

GLAAD—Gay and Lesbian Alliance Against Defamation

Heritage of Pride—The long-time sponsor of the annual Lesbian and Gay Pride Day festivities in New York City.

GAA—Gay Activists' Alliance

. . . and the rest:

The Normal Heart—One of the first plays about the AIDS epidemic to be presented professionally, it holds the record for being the longest-running play in the history of the New York Shakespeare Festival's Public Theater. It was produced in 1985 by the late Joseph Papp, and starred Brad Davis, who died of AIDS-related complications in 1991. The story of the founding of GMHC, *The Normal Heart* also tells the story of how ingrained homophobia within our sociopolitical structure, media, and government allowed the AIDS crisis to spiral into an epidemic.

"Take Back the Street"—A late-night street demonstration and march in June 1990, organized by the newly formed direct-action group Queer Nation, in response to the rise in gay-bashing in the Greenwich Village neighborhoods of New York City. It was attended by over a thousand people, and has taken place annually since then. (It is referred to in this play during "A Thousand Points of Light" as "The Night We Took Back the Street.")